THE LESSER FIELDS

T0164263

The Colorado Prize for Poetry

Strike Anywhere
Dean Young
selected by Charles Simic, 1995

Summer Mystagogia
Bruce Beasley
selected by Charles Wright, 1996

The Thicket Daybreak
Catherine Webster
selected by Jane Miller, 1997

Palma Cathedral
Michael White
selected by Mark Strand, 1998

Popular Music
Stephen Burt
selected by Jorie Graham, 1999

Design
Sally Keith
selected by Allen Grossman, 2000

A Summer Evening
Geoffrey Nutter
selected by Jorie Graham, 2001

Chemical Wedding
Robyn Ewing
selected by Fanny Howe, 2002

Goldbeater's Skin
G. C. Waldrep
selected by Donald Revell, 2003

Whethering
Rusty Morrison
selected by Forrest Gander, 2004

Frayed escort
Karen Garthe
selected by Cal Bedient, 2005

Carrier Wave
Jaswinder Bolina
selected by Lyn Hejinian, 2006

Brenda Is in the Room and Other Poems
Craig Morgan Teicher
selected by Paul Hoover, 2007

One Sun Storm
Endi Bogue Hartigan
selected by Martha Ronk, 2008

The Lesser Fields
Rob Schlegel
selected by James Longenbach, 2009

THE LESSER FIELDS

ROB SCHLEGEL

The Center for Literary Publishing
Colorado State University

For information about permission to reproduce
selections from this book, write to
Permissions, Center for Literary Publishing,
9105 Campus Delivery, Department of English,
Colorado State University,
Fort Collins, Colorado 80523-9105.

Printed in the United States of America.

Library of Congress Cataloging-in-Publication Data

Schlegel, Rob.
The lesser fields / Rob Schlegel.
p. cm. -- (Colorado prize for poetry)
ISBN 978-1-885635-12-9 (pbk. : alk. paper)
I. Title. II. Series.

PS3619.C424L47 2009
811'.6--dc22

2009026329

The paper used in this book meets the minimum requirements of the American
National Standard for Information Sciences-Permanence of Paper for Printed
Library Materials, ANSI Z39.48-1984.

1 2 3 4 5   13 12 11 10 09

for Maxine and Anthony

for Dorothy and Robert

CONTENTS

THE LESSER FIELDS

NOVEMBER DEATHS

LIVES

The moon lying on the brain

                    as on the excited sea   as on
      The strength of fields.   Lord, let me shake
      With purpose.

                        —James Dickey

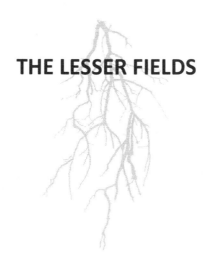

THE LESSER FIELDS

Economy of Winter

Sun peels paint from one side of the vacant house
and the fields turn fallow in the absence of tractors.

A sudden wind disquiets the chimes
and the half-dead cottonwood pays dearly

from its empty pockets; its heavy branches
nod bluntly, threatening nothing but the public road.

Ontogeny

Here and not here, I breathe away
the parts of myself I no longer require.

Would that they return as fish
orbiting globes of algae and every
now and then one might dimple
what I imagine will be my skin—

surface film or epithelium; body I fold
my body into; gravelcloud

and rainstem—a water unending
as the field where I pitch a dozen apples
toward the trunk of a tree until each one

having shattered into many pieces

is a length of horizon by which I measure
where I have not yet happened.

With Shut Eyes What My Mind Sees Does Not Belong to Me

In the city whose streets I knew
by the size of candles kept lit
for the neighbor's missing children

I ate melons in a dusty kitchen
and pierced lures into the lips of fish in my aquarium

until each hook became a leaf
that floated out from the fishes' mouths
and up to the water's surface.

When birds lit on the front lawn
I scared them off with erratic movements.

The voices of my depressed and handsome neighbors
were roughly the same as mine.

Me and not me and the two halves
by the same name.

I lost some people and made a few mistakes.

Each day, I tried to give myself
a different name. Today, you are Jim
I would say, and vertigo might fill your veins

and you will surely lack direction.

Near the freeway entrance
I tried to keep certain thoughts at arm's distance.
I watched a runaway kill snow with urine.

Above him, tiny birds
called out from their common nest.

Icicles Tine Barnward from the Barn's Shallow Eave

Barbwire fence extending field to thicket
from which the flushed birds shed icy shells.

That I should climb each tree before I torch it.

Tongue and bone
abandon me for light resisting alignment.

If this is lament, drown it behind the dam
made with leaves
by the careful feet that mudded them there,
severed now and soldered
to the barn-boards, sun-bleached and split,
this hour into halves stacked in cords.

The fence through which wind blows snow enough
to bury it. Would that I envisage things real
only after I say them so—

against the knife's tip, I slip its pale skin
weight of ash
essential to welcome—

as I dress the bird its feathers scatter.
Ecdysis or wind
in which sound begets particulates of sound
I have not yet lit to watch the flare and flare.

I Pack Her Suitcase with Sticks, Light the Tinder, and Shut the Lid

She used to sit on the forest-floor
and I would cut her hair until it piled up
onto the ground, like ash.

Tonight, her name is a leaf covering
my left eye. The right I close
for the wind to stitch shut with thread

from the dress she wore into the grave
where the determined roots of the tree
are making a braid around her body.

Illuminated Face

From the sidewalks I collect the feathers of birds
murdered by artists
who infuse their paints with the real.

What colors best stain the white beards of men
who mumble at five a.m.
as they wander the streets of America?

As a man, I am free and listening.
As a bird, I am wounded and asleep.

Near the Creek Emptied of Water

Dry-lightning and a thunder made
of needle and pitch—

a sock and its thread a bird found
outside the cabin, the bird

that disturbed the silence—by its feet
I hanged it with thread from the cabin's eave—

and a tally of stains in the curtains.
These should be enough to keep the sick away.

Dusk by Flame

The sudden insects and a shirt tossed onto the pond.

Faceless, the moths trouble nothing but the flame.

Isn't it all—
the before and after of every gesture—remotely elegant?

The barn on fire and the wool of the shirt are trances.

Allies

Until someone steals my coat
I am the younger brother
of each passenger on the train.

I polish their black shoes
and offer to clean the mirrors in every restroom.

At night I sleep and my siblings
try to see the passing fields
by looking out their windows

but the dark glass only reveals
their own reflections

so they think
if they could lighten their hair, they would.

If they could change their names
they would try that too.

Lovemaking in America

I watch a silent film about the sea and I am forced
To imagine the sound the schooner is making.

Upstairs, you fill the bath with everything that has
Or could ever happen between us.

You think you have lived this day before. Earlier
At the fair we found a magician who claimed
He could transport us to a place where the new version of me
Could find the new version of you.

But the magician was only a magician
Whose oldest son took his mother's maiden name.

Somewhere in the future, we are remembering this day
And the wind is gentle over the grass as the old cows
Coddle their young and all of them lift their heavy heads
At the sound of tired people making love.

Secrets Objects Share

Fear is a glass float adrift in the harbor
where my mind breaks
in a weather made by its own waves.

To keep from weeping
I fold paper into paper boats—spinal
increments—the ornamental sterns.

The sea: is it copper or a month of tides
and what they might conceal?

Guardian, give me safe direction.
Release these palms from the public barnacles
and turn this voice into something more
than a scheme of pennies.

I am just a boy weighed down with fear.

Do I sail, or place bluebells
in each vessel named Melissa?

Economy of Winter 2

They might have been olives or grapes
or opulent rows of each, spilling over
the penciled border beneath four or five
cerulean strokes; cumulus loosened
from the sea-dark sky, suffocated

where the paper is wavy
from where you must have paused
to imagine the burdens of composing
within which a drought is composed;
some need within the image itself;

as the tree from which the paper was fashioned
required water, as did the fields
from which the family was fed—

though never enough—when the sun was low
over the house divided
by the single telephone pole,
its endless distance from these dying fields.

Some might say it is the image of a house.
But the house is the image of the tragedies within it.

People Live Here

Alone, she sleeps in this room. Thirty years
since Tony died
and his produce apron still hangs in the closet.

We hunt ghosts seeping out
from mortar between the chimney-brick.

On Division Street, her boy Jerry died
in a red car.

She walks that route with Louise sometimes.

She insists it is bad luck
to match the color of your house
to the color of the house you were born in.

Bad luck to go to sleep stormy.

The windows are open the morning
she first calls me Jerry
and living, she says, is a person at a time.

People gathered here after Jerry died
and the laurel collected a thin layer of dust.

Just wait until after the next rain, she said,
things will look the way they look again.

The Lesser Fields

Are you a branch in the hand of the unwell?
I am a corpse without will.

Are you walking in the field?
I am walking in the field.

Is there a book?
It is the *Book of Woman beneath Water.*

Have you touched the stone?
I have smelled its dry center.

Do you know the flowers?
I know the route to the sea
but the dark waves are resting now.

Are you asleep?

I am salt sorrowing the lesser fields.

NOVEMBER DEATHS

The Snow Uncut Is a Field of Orphans

Whose gardens are shielded with ice

Broken only
By the grosbeaks of winter

She Drops Each Suture from Her Stomach into the Vase on Her Bedside Table

Varnished black
Like the fruit

She tucked beneath a blanket
In the baby cradle

A Boy Is Kicking the Stomach of a Dog

Whose teeth remain private

Whose fate grows heavy this hour
In the morning's frail logic

From a Sheet of Yellow Paper I Cut Bolts of Lightning

To scatter over the birds

Some dead
And some dying

All of them prepared
To return to this world as eyes

If Not a Passage Already Dangerous Then None This Hour Feral with Salt and Rockfish Swiveling Wakes at the Water's Surface as the Strait Swells in the Storm

But for the tip of land
At which the vessel is aimed

There is nothing to steady its course

The Lark's Call Is Smaller than the Field

To see the bird
Open your eyes

A bare branch
Throbbing

A fled bird is
The poem faster

Than its prayer

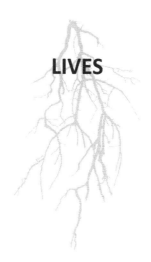

LIVES

Lives of Daughter

The Pacific readies fog
For coastal mountains

As night serves nothing
But sleep and animals
With strong vision.

Around the bulb of a sea iris
I wrap lace from a gown.

Unborn
My daughter is a wave
On the dark ocean.

Lives of Greta

There is that bird again
Finding its way
In transitive flights—

Not fear in the space
Where the rock was
But its fact—

A feeling of if and dirt
In the space where the rock was
A phrase and its refusal.

Then start again.

A feeling of if and a feeling of or

A feeling of and
And a feeling of then

Of where and what more
But when
In life's nonsense

We think of faces
And trembling

Come to see them.

Lives of Tree

The northern saga eyes forest
In seeds

Timbers spinning water
The pond's surface
And oil.

The hill is dark with crickets
Glass bottles keep
When soil emits ink and axle

And thunder stalls the harvest
Mutes the summer
And violets.

Down the tree's creased bark
Lightning starts a seam of heat
Till curtains of flame

Fabric the branches
As flames and the sound of flames

Shape the trees
Burning their first farewell.

Lives of Name

I am in the world, but
With pauses. When I try
To give them context

They call themselves
Coniferous.

All this straining
And to what effect?

I have a name
Someone gave me.

Toward what am I drawn?

That my prayers
Might be forgiven.

That the tallest trees are gods.

Lives of Furrow

My patience is writ
In riddance

In this one page of
A one-page
Letter from loss.

In the pond's still water
What can I see

In sound? The me is me.

I narrate too much.

My hours are buried
In a furrow named Gone.

Lives of Son

Dear Ash Tree, if my son
Cannot find his way
To this world

Replace that desire with limbs
Bending over the weight
Of red berries.

My chore will be a life of harvest
With cold hands. My mouth

A frozen pond
I pray the spring will thaw.

Lives of Empire

Young men sun themselves
In summer's groin

Against the warm root of barter
And the dominant
Become arsonists torching

Iconic sheets from beds
Inhabited by ancestors camped
In the field carved
Into flowers.

The beautiful become unnerving.

Thought and an arm in the grass.

The covey of birds is a palace
Collapsing.

Lives of West

No twitch of the hand goes unnoticed

No turn of the head he fails to respect.
So he learns to ask questions

To look innocent and depleted.

If he sits still, the view always changes
And this is the thinking
He achieves on busses and these
Are his words between dry coughs

California California California.

When I ask him his name he says *Utah.*
Mass production mass production mass
Polygamy. In his mind
I might be naked in honey and bribing horses
By heaving a friendly bulk of hay.

When I ask where he is from
He recalls the name of the one person
Whose face he has touched with his own hand.

Lives of Odin

Who made me is not me
And eating fish
I watch the harbor swell to sea.

On the rich I wish a dozen welts
And a season of unrest
Upon the well-to-do.

Drinking water from the well
I steal the eyes of sleeping giants
And sell them from my pail.

Lives of Lake

To know what Ceres felt
In aster

I become a lake
Through which a fleet of submarines

Is passing—their periscopes
Brightly flashing—

The rain
Pulling my fish from sleep.

Lives of Horse

Limbs leaf out in the orchard
Just opening

And the fog gifts the birds
The horse's back.

Such is beauty
And a belly, sagging
The spine—

A temple or its temperament—
A hoof nearby and buried.

If the lost die lonely
Their skins fill with dirt
And reckoning.

If the wounded die
When the weathers wrap tight
Around neglect

The horses suffer the bridle
Severe and selfless.

Lives of Animal

Stab the night with a shank—
The prettiest metal

Dripping stars. In the body
Cavities of the animals

Arrange a thousand lit candles.

Blink once, then shut your eyes

To see the slaughter.
Custody is in the air. Blink twice

To feel the frost
Sharpen winter's shears
For the smoke of flesh

Its profit and umber ruin.

Lives of Method

Day following day
And the contents add up.

These it is
That clash—then widen

The field of questions—

That which law
And spirit leaven.

Speak the world in multitudes
And stay in it.

Would that every loss
Reveal its science.

That every prayer
Conceal its source.

Lives of Morandi

The color of midnight
Reveals its secrets
As he sews together
His own feet with strands of fiber

Pulled from a canvas
The colors of paint
Have stretched beyond his reach.
With a hammer

He drives a nail into an apple
Which splits
Into a thousand horse-hair narratives.
The forty-acre fields steal water

From the river
Where he washes his shirts
Which he later comes to curse

For bleeding a little crimson
Into his sister's white gowns.

Lives of Rot

The red optimisms
Come to rest in the grove
Where minions volunteer

Maples as reaction.
Fog and the practice of seeds.
The mud is rich with summons

And Rot (tending to her pleasures)
Dips her fingers in water
Till the water aches

For the chronic swell of rivers
Whose stones are drowned birds,
Their silt-filled beaks singing

The strength of light
From a group of stars the prophets
Carved from constellations.

Lives of Modrow

Come around this bedside
She'd say, closer

Yet and look
At these eyes. All her life

She tried to see
The heat of evening

So evening
Is when she died

And left us with what
We might have been to her.

Lives of Nathan

He set out to find
A poultice of red stones in the pond—
Its cool republic of dead leaves

Promising the weird
Perch of music in his ear would ring
Weirder into fever

Till he found a remedy to believe in—
But water in the mouth
Turned deadly in spring

When the pond's promise became
A tangle of duckweed to drown in.

Lives of Cloth

Gravity appeals to the pure
And unjust feast

When humidity
Dulls turbulence in cliffs.

Isolated, the image
Injures the present

And what
But the nostalgia of shawls

To fill holes in the cliff
Abandoned by swallows.

Lives of Forest

On the public ground
I step soft to follow

The one mind of the forest
Whose moss haunts

The limbs of trees that wish
To rid themselves of tariff.

Before my mind
Can shape it, presence

Finishes a thought in my fingers
Such is passage—

A tremble and the fish I touch—

In the dusty shed
Stones on the shelf

Are evidence of mind
In the creek bed

Where salamanders invent
A privacy for sadness.

Lives of Raft

Seeding the shore, pale shells
Wash up the beach

And the dead open their eyes
Stealing sight from birds.

When the ships go out to sea
Their bellows kill the coastal air.

I touch my face with salt
And warm flowers.

On Grief's pier
I brew tea beneath winter's robe.

With dried wood, I build a raft
To capsize alone in the harbor.

Lives of Estuary

Is the dark most complete
Where the restless gather

To convince themselves
Of the ocean? Right now

Are the gods with those
Who are dying? If not, perhaps

They will appear at dawn.

Notes

The epigraph is excerpted from James Dickey, "The Strength of Fields."

"Ontogeny": This poem is for Joanna Klink.

"With Shut Eyes What My Mind Sees Does Not Belong to Me" and **"Secrets Objects Share"**: These poems are for Brandon Shimoda.

"Lovemaking in America": The line "Somewhere in the future I am remembering today" is from David Berman, "The Charm of 5:30."

"The Lesser Fields": "It is the *Book of Woman beneath Water*" is after a line from *Maria Sabina's Selections,* ed. by Jerome Rothenberg and published by the University of California Press. This poem is also indebted to Tomaž Šalamun's "Jonah."

"Lives of Greta": This poem is for the late Greta Wrolstad. ". . . a feeling of if . . ." is indebted to William James.

"Lives of Name": ". . . one is not in the world / but in pauses . . ." is from Michael Davidson, "Screens: 1/28/91."

"Lives of Method": "Love the world and stay inside it" is from Charles Olson, "Maximus, from Dogtown, II."

"Lives of Raft": " . . . and capsized alone in a harbor" is from Tomaž Šalamun, "Academy of American Poets."

Acknowledgements

Thank you to the editors of the following magazines in which these poems first appeared: *Boston Review:* "Icicles Tine Barnward from the Barn's Shallow Eave"; *Harp & Altar:* "Lives of Animal" and "Lives of Tree"; *Leveler:* "With Shut Eyes What My Mind Sees Does Not Belong to Me"; *Mrs. Maybe:* "Lives of Empire" and "Lives of Rot"; and *Puerto del Sol:* "Economy of Winter" and "Ontogeny."

My deep gratitude to James Longenbach and Stephanie G'Schwind.

As ever, I am indebted to my family, friends and teachers; to Kisha.